# I Love DANIEL RADCLIFFE

### Kat Miller

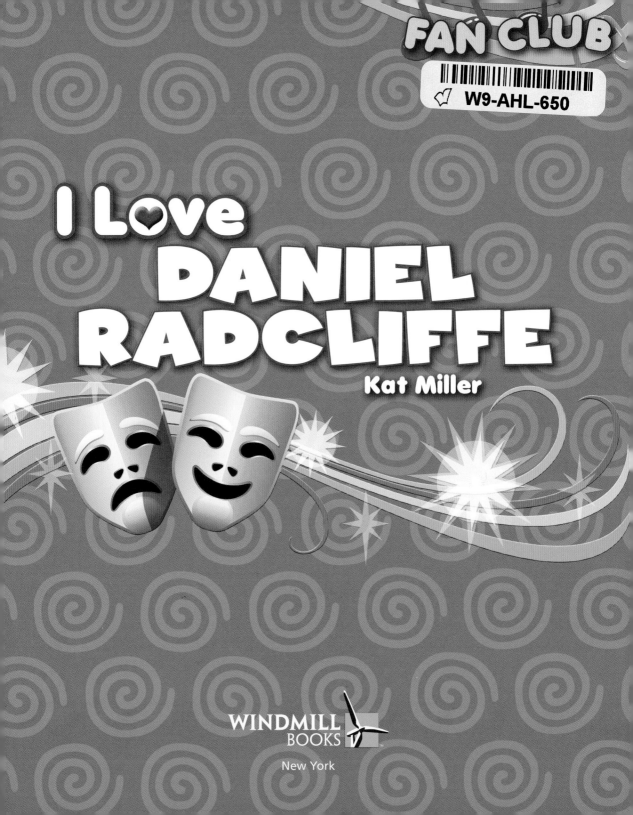

## WINDMILL BOOKS

New York

Published in 2011 by Windmill Books, LLC
303 Park Avenue South, Suite # 1280, New York, NY 10010-3657

Copyright © 2011 by Windmill Books, LLC

CREDITS:
Editor: Jennifer Way
Book Design: Erica Clendening and Greg Tucker
Layout Design: Julio Gil
Photo Research: Ashley Burrell

Photo Credits: Cover Dimitrios Kambouris/WireImage/Getty Images; p. 5 Chris Jackson/Getty Images; pp. 6, 8 (top, bottom), 12, 13, 14 (bottom), 17, 22 Shutterstock.com; p. 7 Dave Hogan/Getty Images; p. 9 Peter Mountain/ WireImage/Getty Images; pp. 10–11 Jim Spellman/WireImage/Getty Images; p. 14 (top) VALERIE MACON/AFP/Getty Images; p. 15 Jeff J Mitchell/Getty Images; pp. 16, 20–21 Bruce Glikas/FilmMagic; p. 18 Eric Charbonneau/ WireImage/Getty Images; p. 19 Tom Shaw/Getty Images.

Library of Congress Cataloging-in-Publication Data
Miller, Kat.
 I love Daniel Radcliffe / by Kat Miller.
     p. cm. — (Fan club)
 Includes bibliographical references and index.
 ISBN 978-1-61533-054-6 (library binding) — ISBN 978-1-61533-055-3 (pbk.) — ISBN 978-1-61533-056-0 (6-pack)
 1. Radcliffe, Daniel, 1989—Juvenile literature. 2. Actors—Great Britain— Biography—Juvenile literature. I. Title.
 PN2598.R27M35 2011
 791.4302'8092—dc22
 [B]
                              2010007045

Manufactured in the United States of America

For more great fiction and nonfiction, go to windmillbooks.com.

CPSIA Compliance Information: Batch #S10W: For further information contact Windmill Books, New York, New York at 1-866-478-0556.

# Contents

# A Much-Loved Actor

Are you a Harry Potter fan? Kids all around the world love the Harry Potter movies. In them, Harry Potter is played by the actor Daniel Radcliffe.

There will be eight Harry Potter movies. Daniel has been playing Harry Potter since 2001. He has found that he has several things in common with Harry.

The Harry Potter movies have been shown around the world. This has made Daniel Radcliffe, seen here, famous in many countries.

Daniel said, "Friendship is very important in both of our lives. I think I have Harry's natural curiosity as well."

# Daniel's Childhood

Daniel Jacob Radcliffe was born in London, England, on July 23, 1989. His parents are Alan Radcliffe and Marcia Gresham. His father was a **literary agent**. His mother casts, or finds actors, for TV shows.

Here is Daniel in 2000. It was taken while he was filming the first Harry Potter movie.

Even as a little kid, Daniel knew that he wanted to act. His first big acting job was in the TV movie *David Copperfield*. The 1999 movie was based on a book by Charles Dickens. Daniel played the young David Copperfield.

Daniel still calls London, seen here, his hometown.

In 2000, Daniel was cast as the lead in the movie *Harry Potter and the Sorcerer's Stone*. The movie was based on the first of a **series** of books about a **wizard** named Harry Potter. Kids around the world read and loved the books.

This is Alan Rickman. He plays Professor Severus Snape in the Harry Potter movies.

PLATFORM 9¾

Here is Daniel in the first Harry Potter movie. In this picture, Harry is holding his pet owl, Hedwig.

Because the books were so loved, the people making the movie knew they had to find the perfect actor to play Harry. Once they met Daniel, they knew that they had found Harry Potter!

Harry and the other students of the Hogwarts School of Witchcraft and Wizardry take a special train to their school that leaves from Platform 9 3/4.

Daniel went on to play Harry Potter for the rest of the movie series. In them, he worked with several different directors. He learned a lot from all of them.

Daniel also got to work with many great actors. Emma Watson and Rupert Grint play Harry's best friends, Hermione and Ron. Daniel, Rupert, and Emma became good

At first, Rupert Grint (left), Emma Watson (middle), and Daniel Radcliffe (right) only signed up for the first few movies. They all ended up acting in all eight movies, though.

friends in real life, too. Daniel also worked with older actors, such as Gary Oldman and Alan Rickman. They gave him **advice** about acting.

# Growing as an Actor

Katie Leung plays Cho Chang, a Hogwarts classmate whom Harry likes.

Over the course of the Harry Potter series, Harry grows up. He has many adventures. He finds out more about his past. He falls in love. He also has to deal with the deaths of people who are important to him.

As he was playing Harry, Daniel was also growing up. He was happy that the later Harry Potter movies offered new acting **challenges**. Daniel's hard work helped him became a better actor.

Daniel goes to the openings of the films he acts in. Here he is in 2005 at the opening of Harry Potter and the Goblet of Fire.

Like the books on which they were based, the Harry Potter movies were huge hits. Millions of people around the world saw them. Together, they made well over a **billion** dollars!

Rupert, Daniel, and Emma got to put their handprints in the sidewalk outside of Grauman's Chinese Theatre in Los Angeles, California.

As the star of a successful movie series, Daniel has been to movie **premieres** all around the world. He has had his picture taken many times. He also gives lots of **interviews**. Daniel meets fans, too. He talks to them and signs **autographs**.

This is what Grauman's Chinese Theatre looks like from the outside.

# Beyond Harry Potter

Though Daniel loves playing Harry Potter, he wants to play other characters, too. In 2007, he appeared in an Australian movie called *December Boys*. He learned to talk with an Australian **accent** for the movie. That same year, he also appeared in the British TV movie *My Boy Jack*.

Here is Daniel with Richard Griffiths. He plays Harry's uncle Vernon Dursley in the Harry Potter movies.

Daniel acted in a play in 2007 and 2008. Daniel saw doing this play as a challenge to himself as an actor.

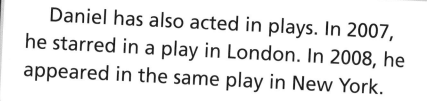

Daniel has also acted in plays. In 2007, he starred in a play in London. In 2008, he appeared in the same play in New York.

The Harry Potter movies have made Daniel rich. However, he does not buy a lot of fancy things. Daniel has used his fame to help others. He has raised money for Demelza Children's Hospice, which cares for sick children.

Daniel likes to watch cricket games. Here he is at a Cricket World Cup match in 2009.

Daniel is a fairly quiet person. He is a big fan of rock music. In fact, Daniel sometimes listens to music to get in the right mood when he is acting. He is also a fan of cricket, a sport that is popular in England.

Daniel is known for making time for his fans. Here, he is meeting with fans at the Sydney, Australia, premiere of *December Boys*.

# What Comes Next?

As of 2010, Daniel is working on *Harry Potter and the Deathly Hallows, Part II*. While there are seven Harry Potter books, there will be eight movies. So much happened in the last book that it had to be made into two movies! The final Harry Potter movie is set to come out in 2011.

Daniel Radcliffe, seen here in 2009, has said he hopes to look for acting challenges after he finishes working on the Harry Potter movies.

Next, Daniel plans to star in a movie about the **photojournalist** Dan Eldon. He will go on playing interesting characters for many years to come.

BROADWAY.COM

2009

Favorite Le... Broadway Play

# Just Like Me!

**1**   Daniel has two pet dogs. Their names are Binka and Nugget. They are both border terriers.

**2**   Daniel has read all of the Harry Potter books. His favorite one was *Harry Potter and the Deathly Hallows*.

**3**   Along with listening to music, some of Daniel's favorite things to do are writing and reading.

**4**   Daniel likes watching movies. Some of his favorites are *12 Angry Men*, *What's Eating Gilbert Grape*, *Rebel Without a Cause*, and *Little Miss Sunshine*.

**5**   In school, Daniel's favorite subject was English. His least favorite subjects were math and French.

# Glossary

**accent** (AK-sent) The way people from a certain place talk.

**advice** (ad-VYS) An opinion about how to handle a problem.

**autographs** (AH-toh-grafs) Copies of person's name, written by that person.

**billion** (BIL-yun) One thousand millions.

**challenges** (CHAH-lun-giz) Things that are hard to do.

**interviews** (IN-ter-vyooz) Times when someone questions someone else.

**literary agent** (LIT-tuh-rahr-ee AY-jent) A person whose job is to act for a writer.

**photojournalist** (foh-toh-JER-nul-ist) A person who takes pictures for a newspaper or magazine.

**premieres** (prih-MYERZ) The first showings of a movie.

**series** (SIR-eez) A group of similar things that come one after another.

**wizard** (WIH-zerd) A person with magical powers.

# Index

# Read More

Rawson, Katherine. *Daniel Radcliffe*. Kid Stars! New York: PowerKids Press, 2009.

Tieck, Sarah. *Daniel Radcliffe*. Big Buddy Biographies. Edina, MA: ABDO, 2010.

Watson, Stephanie. *Daniel Radcliffe: Film and Stage Star*. Hot Celebrity Biographies. Berkeley Heights, NJ: Enslow Publishers, 2009.

# Web Sites

For Web resources related to the subject of this book, go to: www.windmillbooks.com/weblinks and select this book's title.